ACKNOWLEDGEMENTS

Children

Aja M. Gibson, Lisa D. Gibson and Garrick J.D.

Gibson II

I honor the memories my former wife the late

Antoinette L. Burgess

Mother

Rose M. Jeter

Father

Lewis Gibson, Jr.

MORNING MANNA:

Believing God in our tough times will assure us the Victory in the end.

Don't look at what's now but rather what's to come.

What's To Come Will Be Better Than What Has Been!!!!!!!!

NOT A SERMON JUST A THOUGHT!

What Is The True Picture Of Our Reality?

Is it ours or someone else's? Do we own it or rent it? Are we smiling and there's really is a frown inside? What is our reality. To thine own self be true. Let's no longer fake it but rather FIX it.

A Moment Of Transparency and Honesty

"A Moment Of Truth"

I have been feeling a certain kind of way since Friday

I find myself faced with a mixture of emotional feelings that causes me to be angry, frustrated, hurt and yet disappointed. I find myself wondering what could have I don't differently.

Question

What do you do when your past failure continues to attack your mind?

After you. Have prayed after you have read and quoted the word as well as fasted.

I'm dealing with this emotional pain.

Truth of the matter some of us all are dealing with something.

LEAVE IT ALONE AND LET IT GO!!!!!

As I lie in this hospital bed and had 4 Doctors to examine me. A cardiologist, a neurologist and a kidney specialist as they were examining me I heard the spirit of the Lord ask me this question "IS IT WORTH IT" We are carrying around unnecessary things and problems. Put it in the hands of God and let him deal with it. LEAVE IT ALONE AND LET IT GO! IT"S NOT WORTH IT

MORNING MANNA:

Life is like a camera, focus on what is important, capture the good times, develop from the negatives, and if things don't work out, just take another shot. Have A Tremendous Tuesday!

THINGS WILL CHANGE AND GET BETTER!

Never get disgusted with your current location "situation" that's just temporal, but continue to "drive" to your destiny! STAY CONFIDENT! STAY ENCOURAGED! STAY PRAYERFUL! IT CHANGING FOR YOU!

STAY THE COURSE!

Regardless of our plight, situation and circumstances STAY THE COURSE! Through the storm and rain sickness and pain STAY THE COURSE! Sometimes we may feel that we are in it by ourselves, and no-one or no-where to turn but STAY THE COURSE! We are in it to win it so it's a must that we STAY THE COURSE! We must STAY THE COURSE through all. Let us stay faithful to God And true to our struggle "not compromising the integrity of our struggle" because the struggle strengthens and produces divine favor. I ENCOURAGE EVERYONE TO STAY THE COURSE THAT GOD HAS YOU ON. VICTORY IS OUR TO CLAIM!!!!!!

************************STAY THE COURSE*********************

IT'S TIME TO FLY HIGH!!!!!!!

As we prepare to enter into another year let us begin to fly above all things. Let us fly above the hindrances and perplexities of life that we have encountered. Go above it.

MORNING MANNA:

Never allow your temporary situation to become cemented into your future. Everything that you are faced with today does not necessarily mean it is or will be apart of your life. **********The Ministry Of Cutting Off********** Let things go and live!

MORNING MANNA:

JUST DO RIGHT AND LET EVERYTHING ELSE FALL WHERE THEY MAYY!!!!

MORNING MANNA:

Destiny is over my life! Today I encounter my destiny!!!

MORNING MANNA:

THE SAFEST PLACE IN THE WHOLE WORLD IS IN THE WILL OF GOD!!!!!!! Are you in the will of God?

MORNING MANNA:

Family Will Always Be Family And We Can't Change That. But Friends Are A Gift And We Need To Cherish True Friendship!

MORNING MANNA:

FORGIVE QUICKLY, LOVE UNCONDITIONLY, LIVE A STRESS-FREE LIFE AS MUCH AS POSSIBLE! STAND STRONG AND TALL CONTINUE TO HOPE AND DREAM. THINGS WILL WORK OUT!

MORNING MANNA:

PRESSURE BUST PIPES! Please release unnecessary pressure from your life. Pressure causes strokes, heart attacks, break-downs etc. LET IT GO!

MORNING MANNA:

INTENTIONAL SEPARATION BRING CRITICAL CONSECRATION! Thanking God that once you separate and pull away from people and things. God will do that which need to be done in you.

MORNING MANNA:

Moving Forward, Living Better And Being Healthy Is The Order Of The Day! The Greater In You Is Now Ready To Be Experienced. Have A Wonderful Wednesday!

MORNING MANNA:

STAY THE COURSE!

When things go wrong, as they sometime will. When on the road you are troddding seems to be all up hill. DON'T QUIT! JUST STAY THE COURSE! When people may not understand, and friends gets frustrated trust God. JUST STAY THE COURSE! God is developing you in the midst of his Stripping Process. Be determined that you will let God do what he has to do. The process works. Painful but it works My prayer today is Lord don't deliver me out of process but tather take me through it. STAY THE COURSE!

MORNING MANNA:

In order to move forward out of the situation that we are in we must first right the wrong they we have caused. God will not bless us over our wrong. Let us get it right lets repent to God first and ask our brothers and sisters to forgive us.

MORNING MANNA:

YOUR INPATIENCE WILL CAUSE YOU TO BE PATIENT!!! While you are trying to make things move quickly, understand that there can be a lesson in everything that won't move on your time.

SUNDAY MORNING MANNA:

I AM IN GREAT EXPECTATION OF UNCOMMON BLESSING'S AND UNUSUAL FAVOR!!!

MORNING MANNA:

****************2016*************;
** THE YEAR OF DIVINE EXPLOSION!!!
Divine Order Divine Maturity Divine Growth

MORNING MANNA:

LORD MAKE ME A MANAGER OF MY WORD! My desire is to live a life of fulfillment spiritually, naturally and financially. But one the prerequisites is to live a life through the word of God. Watch your words and make sure that the words that you are speaking is grounded in and out of the word of God. Manage Your Words!

MORNING MANNA:

Prioritizing My Priorities! Lord help me to rearrange the things in my life that need to be rearranged and to bring into alignment that which need to be realigned. I'm learning to put first things first..realigned

MORNING MANNA:

YOUR PERSONAL LIBERATION DOESN'T NEED ANY PUBLIC VALIDATION! When the Lord begin to strip you or change something's in your life and brings Liberation don't look for the Validation "approval" of others.

MORNING MANNA:

Sometimes in taking a step forward requires us taking a step back, so we can reevaluate, refocus and realign ourselves on what God wants from us.

MORNING MANNA:

In our lives were faced to make decisions, and in so doing some of our decisions may not be a well liked decision nor an favorable decision. But just make sure that it is a sound decision.

MORNING MANNA:

EVERYONE DIES BUT EVERYONE DOESN'T LIVE! Whatever you do in life be sure not to mishandle that which God has given you. Once it's gone you will regret it. The sting of the pain will be a consent reminder of your mishandling of what God has given you. The tears that fall from your eyes seems to be unstoppable because you are wondering, thinking and reminiscing over your mishandling. Appreciate cherish and gaurd what God has given you and live your life!

MORNING MANNA:

Believe that GOD can and will do what seem to be impossible! Impossible = incapable of existing or occurring, not capable of being accomplished When things seems to be incapable or occurring believe God can cause the impossible thing to happen Look at how God is in the word Impossible I'M Possible God is the I AM in impossibilities

MORNING MANNA:

HE THOUGHT I WAS WORTH SAVING! And because you saved me, I'll give you all the Glory!

MORNING MANNA:

Never allow people or your life situations to change who you are. Praise God through your difficult times and watch God move and change your situations. God will do it.

MORNING MANNA:

Brokenness To Wholeness! God is moving us to a place of Wholeness! Healing us from the pain hurt and devastation. No longer allow yourself to operate in brokenness but walk in the faith of God and become WHOLE MORNING MANNA: If we would really pay attention and listen to God when he speaks to us and do what he say. We would be better prepared and ready to move when he opens doors for us to walk through.
#readytowalkinthedoors

MORNING MANNA:

He Loved Me Because Of He saved me In spite Of and for that I am eternally thankful!

MORNING MANNA:

GOD IS FAITHFUL TO HIS WORD! Faith + Works make Impossibilities, Possible.

MORNING MANNA:

If You Keep Wisdom, Wisdom Will Keep You! Pastor Tammy Williams

MORNING MANNA:

Great maturity in and of life can help process and heal from great pain and devastating hurt that we have experienced. Allow our maturity to guide us through the crisis, concerns and the cares, of our life's experience.

MORNING MANNA:

The process does not have to be stressful! Be consistent in the midst of your process! Don't faint in the midst of your process. Focus yourself on the end knowing that you going to win. God will redeem the time for us. God will sustain us through this or that.

MORNING MANNA:

Never allow anyone or anything to encage you or minimize you. There is Divine Greatness in you and upon you. Do not live you life based on someone else's ideas and thoughts of what you should do. I employ you to explore and develop that seed of greatness that God has imparted into you. Let us cultivate, nourish our seed to maturity. In other words let us in enlarge our territory. Have A Faithful Friday!

MORNING MANNA:

Small Changes Can Bring Big Results! Who wants big results? Start with the the small.

MORNING MANNA:

EXPECTATION IS YOUR BREEDING GROUND FOR YOUR MIRACLE! Believe it you'll Receive It But if you Doubt It you'll Do Without It!

MORNING MANNA:

Sometimes in our life one needs to step back to examine it. We need to be mindful that if we are going to grow then we must relieve ourselves of deadly and toxic things. Sisters and brothers in my prayer time this morning the Lord said to me RELEASE YOURSELF! Have your ever gotten to involved in people and things that it messed up the course of your life? Please let things go. Find out who you are and live for you. Here's the questions to ask yourself 1) Am I living my joy or living someone else's 2) Am I living someone else's dream or am I building my dream. 3) Am I being fulfilled while I am I helping to fulfill others. Having said that I realized that I must stop count my loss and START OVER. Yes start over from the beginning. Starting all over again! We get caught up in helping in building other until we forget about outselves *******IT'S ROUGH BUT NECESSARY *******

MORNING MANNA:

The stripping process of starting over is a very PAINFUL experience! You literary feel the pulling away the detachment of thing from you. Trust when I tell you that you cannot take any pain reliever that will keep you from feeling this pain. But I must endure because the end of this is worth it all. Let God Strip You!

Morning Manna

Never Allow Anyone To Make You A Good Option. When You Can Be A great Priority. When you are an OPTION then you will set yourself up to be used, abused and misused. When you are the PRIORITY you will be honored and esteemed. Use this in EVERY aspect of your life.

MORNING MANNA:

NEVER FLY BLINDLY, JUST FLY BY FAITH!!!!!!

MORNING MANNA:

Lord, help me leave hesitation alone today, and charge forward into the future that you've ordained for my life. Hear God For The Next Move Of Our Life Then Move Forward!!!

MORNING MANNA:

THE ONLY WAY TO AVOID CRITICISM, IS TO SAY NOTHING, DO NOTHING, AND BE NOTHING. Do something!

MORNING MANNA:

WHAT CHOICE ARE YOU MAKING? To live a life of freedom is a choice! You must choose to be Healthy. You must choose to have peace. You must choose to have a piece of mind. It's Up To You!

MORNING MANNA|

THERE IS ALWAYS A PURPOSE BEHIND YOUR PROBLEM! As of today look at your problems in a different way. Understand the problems that you are facing can be used to propel you into the purpose that God has for your life Don't dismiss your pain but deal with it. Examine your problem and pursue your God-given purpose

NOT A SERMON JUST MY THOUGHT:

Let your conviction be based on and in the Word of God and not your emotions.

Saints our emotion need to yield to the Word of God!!!!!

NOT A SERMON JUST MY THOUGHT:

If you are the smartest person in your group. Then it's time to evolve and get a new group.

Never allow yourself to stay stunted in any environment. Growth is a must.

NOT A SERMON JUST MY THOUGHT:

Your past can be holding your future back. So Let it go it's not worth what's before you.

NOT A SERMON JUST MY THOUGHT:

I Declare And Decree that

Something GOOD Is Coming You Way. Something GOOD Is Going To Happen To You!

SO WHY NOT PUT A PRAISE ON IT!!!!!!!

Can someone just touch and agree and type PRAISE ON IT!!!!

Oh God I Got A Praise On It!!!!!!!!!!!!!!!!!!!

NOT A SERMON JUST MY THOUGHT:

Destiny is over our lives! Today will you prepare for the encounter of your Destiny!!

NOT A SERMON JUST MY THOUGHT:

KNOW WHO YOU ARE!!!!!

Just because others don't see your WHY/PURPOSE don't mean you don't have one. Jesse had a king in his house named David, and didn't know it.

Have A Favorable Friday Facebook!

NOT A SERMON JUST MY THOUGHT:

Moving Forward Without Any Exceptions!

Joy is yours to claim! Destiny is yours to secure! Peace is yours to walk in.

Forgetting your past, celebrate your now and prepare to enjoy your future.

Bless you Facebook.

NOT A SERMON JUST MY THOUGHT:

WHAT'S ON YOUR MIND?

The best way to maintain a clear mind is to know the mind of Christ by meditating often of His Word.

What are you filling your mind with?

NOT A SERMON JUST MY THOUGHT:

"FORGIVENESS IS A MUST!

Holding onto unforgivness is like you drinking poison, and expecting the other person to die. It only harms you, not them.

NOT A SERMON JUST MY THOUGHT:

YOUR INPATIENCE WILL CAUSE YOU TO BE PATIENT!!!

While you are trying to make things move quickly, understand that there can be a lesson in everything that won't move on your time.

NOT A SERMON JUST MY THOUGHT:

EXPECTATION IS THE BREEDING GROUND FOR YOUR MIRACLE!!!!!!

Believe It You'll Receive It, Doubt It You'll Do Without It.

NOT A SERMON JUST MY THOUGHT:

STAY THE COURSE!

When things go wrong, as they sometime will. When on the road you are troddding seems to be all up hill. DON'T QUIT!

JUST STAY THE COURSE!

People may not understand, and friends may even get frustrated but trust God.

JUST STAY THE COURSE!

God is developing you in the midst of his Stripping Process. Be determined that you will let God do what he has to do. The process works. It's painful but it works

My prayer today is Lord don't deliver me out/from the process but rather take me through it.

STAY THE COURSE!

NOT A SERMON JUST MY THOUGHT:

BROKENNESS TO WHOLENESS!

God is moving us to a place of Wholeness! Healing us from the pain hurt and devastation.

No longer allow yourself to operate in brokenness but walk in the faith of God and become WHOLE.

NOT A SERMON JUST MY THOUGHT:

Success Isn't given to anyone to hold that's not prepared.

PREPARATION IS EVERYTHING!!!

PREPARE TO SUCCEED!!!

NOT A SERMON JUST MY THOUGHT:

Lord Allow Me To Expand My Capacity So You Can Expand My Territory!!!!

Saints while we are asking God to give us territory we should also ask God first to give us the the imagination/vision to hold on secure the territory that he gives us.

It's one thing to acquire it but it's another thing to get purpose from it.

Kingdom Blessings To You!

NOT A SERMON JUST MY THOUGHT:

When you have done all that you could, and things just won't /dont work in your favor learn to back up and leave it alone.

Back up and back off because you just may need to focus and direct your attention elsewhere.

Not A SERMON JUST MY THOUGHT:

YOU WILL MAKE IT BECAUSE THINGS WILL WORK OUT! Romans 8:28

When I awoke this morning the Lord told me to encourage my people and let them know that I am with them through this tempestuous time.

That what looks like defeat will turn to be your VICTORY.

NOT A SERMON JUST MY THOUGHT:

Sometimes in order to move forward one must probably need to take a step back.

Take time to step back to realign, reassess, reevaluate, and refocus.than we can move forward.

NOT A SERMON JUST MY THOUGHT:

LIVE LIFE TO ITS MAXIMUM!

Live your life and don't allow your life to live you. Whatever you may be faced or challenged with DON'T let it control your life.

Jesus said that I come that you may have life and that more abundantly.

I speak this into someone today "Begin Living ". You can live beyond your crisis, chaos and confusion.

IT'S TIME TO LIVE!!!!!!!

NOT A SERMON JUST MY THOUGHT:

When people counted you out, remember that God has counted you in.

Know and believe that you can make it!

NOT A SERMON JUST MY THOUGHT:

No longer must we strategize through our own opinion or intellect. But we must strategize through prayer and the word of God!

Allow the word of God to take you into your new place. The place of refreshing and renewal.

NOT A SERMON JUST A THOUGHT:

IT"S A NEW DAY SO LET IT BE A NEW MINDSET!

NOT A SERMON JUST MY THOUGHT:

Walking Away From A Thing Can Be Painful And Uncomfortable. But Understand Where You Are Going Is Much Better Than Where You Have Been.

Trust God In Your Process!!!

NOT A SERMON JUST MY THOUGHT:

New brooms sweep clean but the old broom knows/fits the corners!

Don't forget about the people that was with you in hard and difficult times when new people come along. Because the old people knows you.

NOT A SERMON JUST MY THOUGHT:

WHY LIVE A LIE WHEN YOU CAN LIVE IN PEACE!

WHOM THE son hath made free is free INDEED.

NOT A SERMON JUST MY THOUGHT:

Sin is like a credit card, easy to use but hard to pay off.

Think about it.

NOT A SERMON JUST MY THOUGHT:

GROW THROUGH WHAT YOU GO THROUGH!

Life has a way of throwing you a few curve, and uncertainties have attempted to arrest your mind.

Life is a one way street, from the cradle to the grave. There's no time outs there's no intermission but it's a steady progression from the Date of Birth until The Date of Death.

Whatever the situation maybe in your life know that it is a lesson to be learned. It may be painful but endure the lesson. Grow through it.

Jul 7

NOT A SERMON JUST MY THOUGHT:

Whatever We Do This Question Needs To Be Asked.

Is God Satisfied With My Motives And My Intentions.

Whatever you do please do it from a PURE PLACE.

NOT A SERMON JUST MY THOUGHT:

The next move of God in your life will be EPIC!!!!!

Get ready for the Move because it's on the way.

NOT A SERMON JUST MY THOUGHT:

Regardless of the the downs of life and the hardships that we may be experiencing. Never get tired of pursuing your God Given Destiny and Dreams.

Keep chasing and running after it, God will strengthen you. God allow RESETS!

NOT A SERMON JUST MY THOUGHT:

YOUR PERSONAL LIBERATION DOESN'T NEED ANY PUBLIC VALIDATION!

When the Lord begins to strip, change or redirect something's in your life and brings Liberation don't look for the Validation "approval" of others.

Thanking God For The Move Of Liberation!

NOT A SERMON JUST MY THOUGHT:

Love God, Love Yourself, Intentionally Forgive, Laugh often and Live Life To The Fullest!! Be Blessed!!

Love Isn't Love Unless You Can Give It Away!

NOT A SERMON JUST MY THOUGHT:

Take time to love on those that are in your life. Never take them for granted.

Support, love and celebrate one another and thank God for those that's in your life.

NOT A SERMON JUST MY THOUGHT:

There come times in our lives when we must step back and assess the damage that's in our life. As we begin the process to repair the damages that's in our lives that can prove to be very problematic for us. Let us rebuild on the word of God.

NOT A SERMON JUST MY THOUGHT:

NEVER FLY BLINDLY, JUST FLY BY FAITH!!!!!!

NOT A SERMON JUST MY THOUGHT:

When in doubt, confusion and bewilderment learn to trust God's word.

Believe and know that God's word will never fail. The situation may look as it will fail but know God has it.

NOT A SERMON JUST MY THOUGHT:

HOLINESS IS STILL THE ORDER OF THE DAY!!!!!!!!!!

HOW ARE YOU LIVING?

NOT A SERMON JUST MY THOUGHT:

Well I'm feeling mighty happy, feeling mighty fine I'm enjoying JESUS Hallelujah!!!!!!!!!

NOT A SERMON JUST MY THOUGHT:

"PREPERATION IS EVERYTHING"

If we would really pay attention and listen to God when he speaks to us and do what he say. We would be better prepared and ready to move when he opens doors for us to walk through.

NOT A SERMON JUST MY THOUGHT:

When You Are In The Right Place, God knows How To Get The Resource That You Need To You.

Live Right, Live Truthful And Live Whole!

NOT A SERMON JUST MY THOUGHT!

WHEN THINGS ARE WORKING REMEMBER IT"S GOD DOING THE WORK!!!!!!!

NOT A SERMON JUST MY THOUGHT:

"THINGS WILL CHANGE AND GET BETTER!"

Never get disgusted with your current location "situation" that's just temporal, but continue to "drive" to your destiny!

STAY CONFIDENT! STAY ENCOURAGED! STAY PRAYERFUL!

IT CHANGING FOR YOU!

NOT A SERMON JUST MY THOUGHT:

I Believe God, I Believe God, I Believe God Will Do What He Say.

Trust And Obey There's No Other Way I Believe I Believe God.

Believe It You'll Receive It But If You Doubt It You Will Do Without It.

NOT A SERMON JUST MY THOUGHT:

EVERYTHING RESTS IN THE HAND OF THE LORD!!!!

Put it in his hands.

NOT A SERMON JUST MY THOUGHT:

GOD IS FAITHFUL TO HIS WORD AND HIS PEOPLE.

Faith + Works makes Impossibilities, Possible.

Sept 20

NOT A SERMON JUST MY THOUGHT:

WE SHALL WIN! WE EXPECT TO WIN! WE WILL WIN!

There is a WIN in my spirit. We are WINNERS!

Not A SERMON JUST MY THOUGHT:

A New Day, A New Mindset Brimgs About A Fresh Start!

Who needs It?

NOT A SERMON JUST MY THOUGHT:

THE RE'S IN MY LIFE

RENEW, REBUILD, RECOMMIT, REDEDICATE, REFOCUS, RESTORE and to RETHINK my life.

If change is to take place then you must do something different.

FRESH START!

NOT A SERMON JUST MY THOUGHT:

"CHANGE RENDERS RESULTS"

IF WE WANT CHANGE IN OUR LIVES THEN SOMETIMES WE MUST MAKE SOME RADICAL CHANGES WITHIN OURSELVES!!!!!

CHANGE REQUIRES DISCIPLINE, DISCIPLINE REQUIRES DETERMINATION, DETERMINATION REQUIRES DIRECTION TO KNOW WHERE YOU WANT TO GO IN YOUR CHANGE.

NOT A SERMON JUST MY THOUGHT:

NO ENEMIES NO TABLE! Psalm 23:5

Your enemies will be the cause that you eat royally

NOT A SERMON JUST MY THOUGHT:

NEVER ALLOW YOURSELF TO FIT IN SOMEONE ELSE'S FRAMEWORK/BOX.

BE A TRENDSETTER!

NOT A SERMON JUST MY THOUGHT:

A NEW DAY A NEW MINDSET!!!

Yesterday some was hurt, yesterday some was drained. Yesterday some had to face uncertainties of situations.

But today is another New Day and we ain't gone, and realize that the Lord has kept us thru the calamities, hurt, pain and frustrations of yesterday. It's A NEW DAY!

A NEW DAY brings a NEW Thought, NEW

Day brings NEW COURAGE. But most of all A NEW MINDSET!

IT'S GETTING BETTER ALL THE TIME!

NOT A SERMON JUST MY THOUGHT:

I would rather someone tell me the ugly truth, than a pretty lie.

Am I not your friend because I told you the truth?

NOT A SERMON JUST MY THOUGHT:

Don't work more on our calling than you do on our character. Many people are a public success but a private failure because they work more on their calling than they do on their. character. The more we work on our character and integrity, the better our life will be. Our character will protect our calling.

2018 THE YEAR OF DIVINE ORDER!

NOT A SERMON JUST MY THOUGHT:

I AM A POSITIVE THINKER!!! Bishop C.L. Long

No matter your plight think positive. God has a set time to bring you out.

I AM A POSITIVE THINKER!!!!!

NOT A SERMON JUST MY THOUGHT:

Faith Based, Faith Walking, Faith Living

Living My Expectations Through Faith. Hab 2:4

NOT A SERMON JUST MY THOUGHT:

GOD ALTERS YOUR LIFE PLANNED EVENTS!

Have you ever had anything planned and while you was in pursuit of just to find what you planned is not your plans any longer.

Have you ever planned a certain career and was working on it, just to find yourself in a total different career.

Have you ever said that you wasn't going to do something, but you find yourself doing that which you said you wouldn't do.

GOD ALTERS YOUR LIFE PLANNED EVENTS!

NOT A SERMON JUST MY THOUGHT:

Life doesn't come with a remote control. If you don't like what you're seeing, get up and change it

NOT A SERMON JUST MY THOUGHT:

LORD GIVE ME THE STRENGTH TO SELF EMPTY!

Everything that's not like you, Lord strengthen me to let it Go.

Pride, bitterness, unforgiveness, doubt, fear and etc. I self empty and give it up.

Self Empty!!!!!!!

NOT A SERMON JUST MY THOUGHT:

Never Allow Your Temporary Situation To Become Cemented Into Your Coming Future.

Everything that you are faced with today does not necessarily mean it is or will be apart of your life.

**********The Ministry Of Cutting Off**********

Let things go and live!

NOT A SERMON JUST MY THOUGHT:

DON'T COMPROMISE THE INTEGRITY OF THE PROCESS!

Don't get distracted by the process of change. Stay until the change is complete!! Once transformed, you'll never go back.... A butterfly can't go back to a caterpillar!

NOT A SERMON JUST MY THOUGHT:

GOD HAS IT ALL IN CONTROL!

God Alters life planned events.

Thank you God for intervening.

NOT A SERMON JUST MY THOUGHT:

GOD IS NOT BROKE AND THE ANGELS ARE NOT ON WELFARE!

Believe God and will work it out!

NOT A SERMON JUST MY THOUGHT:

A GOOD IDEA DOES NOT MEAN THAT IT'S A GOD IDEA!

SEEK GOD Proverbs 3:5-7

NOT A SERMON JUST MY THOUGHT:

Through Your Life's Story, Don't Ever Forget To Give God The Glory!

NOT A SERMON JUST MY THOUGHT

last post will be on October 31st. My prayer is that someone had been blessed over the last 11 years with the daily inspiration.

Please be on the lookout for the book "Morning Dew" which is a book that will have excerpts from Not A Sermon Just My Thought.

Have a good night tonight and a better day tomorrow.

NOT A SERMON JUST MY THOUGHT:

DON'T ALLOW THE TROUBLE TO TROUBLE YOU,

BUT RATHER TROUBLE YOUR TROUBLE!

NOT A SERMON JUST MY THOUGHT:

STOP TELLING PEOPLE WHERE YOU ARE GOING, BUT RATHER START TELLING THEM WHERE YOU HAVE BEEN!

In other words don't tell people what you are going to do but what you have done.

NOT A SERMON JUST MY THOUGHT:

MY EXPECTED END IS DESIGNED BY GOD!

Jeremiah 29:11

NOT A SERMON JUST MY THOUGHT:

Hear God's Voice Clearly And Follow His Instructions Closely!!!

NOT A SERMON JUST MY THOUGHT:

IT'S OK TO CROSSOVER AS LONG AS YOU TAKE THE CROSS WITH YOU!

NOT A SERMON JUST MY THOUGHT:

GRACE FOR YOUR SITUATION!

Regardless of your plight, situation and circumstances remember that God's Grace can be found in the midst of your situation

NOT A SERMON JUST MY THOUGHT:

God Is Bringing It All Together!

Step Back And Watch Him Do It.

NOT A SERMON JUST MY THOUGHT:

FAITH LIVING!

BELIEVE IT YOU'LL RECEIVE IT, BUT IF YOU DOUBT IT YOU'LL DO WITHOUT IT!

NOT A SERMON JUST MY THOUGHT:

MOVING FROM A LIFE OF SURVIVAL TO A LIFE OF SUCCESS! JER. 29:11

NOT A SERMON JUST MY THOUGHT:

A PRAISE THAT EXCITES GOD!!!

DO YOU HAVE ONE?

NOT A SERMON JUST MY THOUGHT:

MOVING FORWARD UNAPOLOGETICALLY AND WITHOUT REGRET!!!!!!

WHAT'S TO COME IS BETTER THAN WHAT HAS BEEN.

NEVER ALLOW YOURSELF TO BE TOLERATED WHEN YOU CAN BE CELEBRATED!

MOVE FORWARD AND LIVE!

NOT A SERMON JUST MY THOUGHT:

HOLINESS IS STILL THE ORDER OF THE DAY!!!!!!!!!!

HOW ARE YOU LIVING?

NOT A SERMON JUST MY THOUGHT:

Well I'm feeling mighty happy, feeling mighty fine I'm enjoying JESUS Hallelujah!!!!!!!!!

NOT A SERMON JUST MY THOUGHT:

"PREPERATION IS EVERYTHING"

If we would really pay attention and listen to God when he speaks to us and do what he say. We would be better prepared and ready to move when he opens doors for us to walk through.

NOT A SERMON JUST MY THOUGHT:

When You Are In The Right Place, God knows How To Get The Resource That You Need To You.

Live Right, Live Truthful And Live Whole!

NOT A SERMON JUST MY THOUGHT!

WHEN THINGS ARE WORKING REMEMBER IT"S GOD DOING THE WORK!!!!!!!

NOT A SERMON JUST MY THOUGHT:

"THINGS WILL CHANGE AND GET BETTER!"

Never get disgusted with your current location "situation" that's just temporal, but continue to "drive" to your destiny!

STAY CONFIDENT! STAY ENCOURAGED! STAY PRAYERFUL!

IT CHANGING FOR YOU!

NOT A SERMON JUST MY THOUGHT:

I Believe God, I Believe God, I Believe God Will Do What He Say.

Trust And Obey There's No Other Way I Believe I Believe God.

Believe It You'll Receive It But If You Doubt It You Will Do Without It.

NOT A SERMON JUST MY THOUGHT:

EVERYTHING RESTS IN THE HAND OF THE LORD!!!!

Put it in his hands.

NOT A SERMON JUST MY THOUGHT:

GOD IS FAITHFUL TO HIS WORD AND HIS PEOPLE.

Faith + Works makes Impossibilities, Possible.

NOT A SERMON JUST MY THOUGHT:

WE SHALL WIN! WE EXPECT TO WIN! WE WILL WIN!

There is a WIN in my spirit. We are WINNERS!

Not A SERMON JUST MY THOUGHT:

A New Day, A New Mindset Brimgs About A Fresh Start!

Who needs It?

NOT A SERMON JUST MY THOUGHT:

THE RE'S IN MY LIFE

RENEW, REBUILD, RECOMMIT, REDEDICATE, REFOCUS, RESTORE and to RETHINK my life.

If change is to take place then you must do something different.

FRESH START!

NOT A SERMON JUST MY THOUGHT:

"CHANGE RENDERS RESULTS"

IF WE WANT CHANGE IN OUR LIVES THEN SOMETIMES WE MUST MAKE SOME RADICAL CHANGES WITHIN OURSELVES!!!!!

CHANGE REQUIRES DISCIPLINE, DISCIPLINE REQUIRES DETERMINATION, DETERMINATION REQUIRES DIRECTION TO KNOW WHERE YOU WANT TO GO IN YOUR CHANGE.

NOT A SERMON JUST MY THOUGHT:

Never allow life's problems to overshadow the PURPOSE AND PRINCIPLES for your life through God's word.

NOT A SERMON JUST MY THOUGHT:

NO ENEMIES NO TABLE! Psalm 23:5

Your enemies will be the cause that you eat royally

NOT A SERMON JUST MY THOUGHT:

NEVER ALLOW YOURSELF TO FIT IN SOMEONE ELSE'S FRAMEWORK/BOX.

BE A TRENDSETTER!

NOT A SERMON JUST MY THOUGHT:

A NEW DAY A NEW MINDSET!!!

Yesterday some was hurt, yesterday some was drained. Yesterday some had to face uncertainties of situations.

But today is another New Day and we ain't gone, and realize that the Lord has kept us thru the calamities, hurt, pain and frustrations of yesterday. It's A NEW DAY!

A NEW DAY brings a NEW Thought, NEW

Day brings NEW COURAGE. But most of all A NEW MINDSET!

IT'S GETTING BETTER ALL THE TIME!

NOT A SERMON JUST MY THOUGHT:

I would rather someone tell me the ugly truth, than a pretty lie.

Am I not your friend because I told you the truth?

NOT A SERMON JUST MY THOUGHT:

Don't work more on our calling than you do on our character. Many people are a public success but a private failure because they work more on their calling than they do on their. character. The more we work on our character and integrity, the better our life will be. Our character will protect our calling.

2018 THE YEAR OF DIVINE ORDER!

NOT A SERMON JUST MY THOUGHT:

I AM A POSITIVE THINKER!!! Bishop C.L. Long

No matter your plight think positive. God has a set time to bring you out.

I AM A POSITIVE THINKER!!!!!

NOT A SERMON JUST MY THOUGHT:

Faith Based, Faith Walking, Faith Living

Living My Expectations Through Faith.
Hab 2:4

NOT A SERMON JUST MY THOUGHT:

GOD ALTERS YOUR LIFE PLANNED EVENTS!

Have you ever had anything planned and while you was in pursuit of just to find what you planned is not your plans any longer.

Have you ever planned a certain career and was working on it, just to find yourself in a total different career.

Have you ever said that you wasn't going to do something, but you find yourself doing that which you said you wouldn't do.

GOD ALTERS YOUR LIFE PLANNED EVENTS!

NOT A SERMON JUST MY THOUGHT:

Life doesn't come with a remote control. If you don't like what you're seeing, get up and change it

NOT A SERMON JUST MY THOUGHT:

LORD GIVE ME THE STRENGTH TO SELF EMPTY!

Everything that's not like you, Lord strengthen me to let it Go.

Pride, bitterness, unforgiveness, doubt, fear and etc. I self empty and give it up.

Self Empty!!!!!!!

NOT A SERMON JUST MY THOUGHT:

Never Allow Your Temporary Situation To Become Cemented Into Your Coming Future.

Everything that you are faced with today does not necessarily mean it is or will be apart of your life.

*****The Ministry Of Cutting Off**********

Let things go and live!

NOT A SERMON JUST MY THOUGHT:

DON'T COMPROMISE THE INTEGRITY OF THE PROCESS!

Don't get distracted by the process of change. Stay until the change is complete!! Once transformed, you'll never go back…. A butterfly can't go back to a caterpillar!

NOT A SERMON JUST MY THOUGHT:

GOD HAS IT ALL IN CONTROL!

God Alters life planned events.

Thank you God for intervening.

NOT A SERMON JUST MY THOUGHT:

GOD IS NOT BROKE AND THE ANGELS ARE NOT ON WELFARE!

Believe God and will work it out!

NOT A SERMON JUST MY THOUGHT:

A GOOD IDEA DOES NOT MEAN THAT IT'S A GOD IDEA!

SEEK GOD Proverbs 3:5-7

NOT A SERMON JUST MY THOUGHT:

Through Your Life's Story, Don't Ever Forget To Give God The Glory!

NOT A SERMON JUST MY THOUGHT

last post will be on October 31st. My prayer is that someone had been blessed over the last 11 years with the daily inspiration.

Please be on the lookout for the book "Morning Dew" which is a book that will have excerpts from Not A Sermon Just My Thought.

Have a good night tonight and a better day tomorrow.

NOT A SERMON JUST MY THOUGHT:

DON'T ALLOW THE TROUBLE TO TROUBLE YOU,

BUT RATHER TROUBLE YOUR TROUBLE!

NOT A SERMON JUST MY THOUGHT:

STOP TELLING PEOPLE WHERE YOU ARE GOING, BUT RATHER START TELLING THEM WHERE YOU HAVE BEEN!

In other words don't tell people what you are going to do but what you have done.

NOT A SERMON JUST MY THOUGHT:

MY EXPECTED END IS DESIGNED BY GOD!

Jeremiah 29:11

NOT A SERMON JUST MY THOUGHT:

Hear God's Voice Clearly And Follow His Instructions Closely!!!

NOT A SERMON JUST MY THOUGHT:

IT'S OK TO CROSSOVER AS LONG AS YOU TAKE THE CROSS WITH YOU!

NOT A SERMON JUST MY THOUGHT:

GRACE FOR YOUR SITUATION!

Regardless of your plight, situation and circumstances remember that God's Grace can be found in the midst of your situation

NOT A SERMON JUST MY THOUGHT:

God Is Bringing It All Together!

Step Back And Watch Him Do It.

NOT A SERMON JUST MY THOUGHT:

FAITH LIVING!

BELIEVE IT YOU'LL RECEIVE IT, BUT IF YOU DOUBT IT YOU'LL DO WITHOUT IT!

NOT A SERMON JUST MY THOUGHT:
MOVING FROM A LIFE OF SURVIVAL TO A LIFE OF SUCCESS! JER. 29:11

NOT A SERMON JUST MY THOUGHT:

A PRAISE THAT EXCITES GOD!!!

DO YOU HAVE ONE?

NOT A SERMON JUST MY THOUGHT:

MOVING FORWARD UNAPOLOGETICALLY AND

WITHOUT REGRET!!!!!!

WHAT'S TO COME IS BETTER THAN WHAT HAS BEEN.

NEVER ALLOW YOURSELF TO BE TOLERATED WHEN YOU CAN BE CELEBRATED!

MOVE FORWARD AND LIVE!

NOT A SERMON JUST MY THOUGHT:

LOOK AGAIN!!!

The good news is that the bad news was wrong.

NOT A SERMON JUST MY THOUGHT:

THE ONLY WAY TO AVOID CRITICISM, IS TO SAY NOTHING, DO NOTHING, AND BE NOTHING.

Do something!!!

NOT A SERMON JUST MY THOUGHT:

GOD IS GOING TO GET US THROUGH THIS.

RECOVERY!!!

NOT A SERMON JUST MY THOUGHT:

True Repentance

Produces True Humility.

The Way To Go Up Is To Go Low.

NOT A SERMON JUST MY THOUGHT:

When You Are In The Right Place, God knows How To Get The Resource That You Need To You.

Live Right, Live Truthful And Live Whole!

NOT A SERMON JUST MY THOUGHT:

STEP BACK, REASSESS AND REALIGN.

NOT A SERMON JUST MY THOUGHT:

If You Keep Wisdom, Wisdom Will Keep You!

Let us operate in wisdom.

NOT A SERMON JUST MY THOUGHT:

GOD ISN'T IN THE COMPLAINANT BUSINESS!

Stop complaining about your problems and thank him for protecting you.

NOT A SERMON JUST MY THOUGHT:

HAVE A GOOD AND GREAT DAY, BELIEVE AND KNOW YOU DESERVE IT!

TODAY I WON'T ENTERTAIN FOOLISHNESS.

NOT A SERMON JUST MY THOUGHT:

Moving From A Painful Process To A Prolific Promise!

NOT A SERMON JUST MY THOUGHT:

Prepared and Positioned To Receive The Promise!

NOT A SERMON JUST MY THOUGHT:

EVERYTHING Is Working Out For Me!

Make this your daily confession.

NOT A SERMON JUST MY THOUGHT!

DON'T EXPECT GOD'S DIRECTION IF YOU CAN'T ACCEPT GOD'S CORRECTION.

NOT A SERMON JUST MY THOUGHT:

Sometimes You Gotta Give Up The Power in Order To Gain The Control.

NOT A SERMON JUST MY THOUGHT:

LORD I THANK YOU FOR NOT PARALYZING MY TOUNGE! So On That Note I Will Praise Your Name.

NOT A SERMON JUST MY THOUGHT:

MOVING FORWARD WITHOUT ANY FURTHER DELAYS.

DESTINY AWAITS US!

NOT A SERMON JUST MY THOUGHT:

When We Possess The Attitude Of A Student, We Can Remain Teachable!

NOT A SERMON JUST MY THOUGHT:

ANOITED or ARROGANT

Which One Describes You?

MORNING MANNA:

Honor will get you into places with people that dishonor will not permit you to enter. Let's restore honor and honor one another.. IT"S JUST NICE TO BE NICE!

MORNING MANNA:

PROVE YOURSELF TO YOURSELF!!!!!!! On today make up your mind that you will be the Best In Yourself. Knowing that you have nothing to prove to anyone but yet all to prove to yourself. We have been so busy trying to prove ourselves to other people to get their approval. When all along we have a lot to prove to ourselves. Let's make up our minds that we will change, turn around and soar to Heights unknown. That we will do it not to show anybody else nor to try to prove to anybody else but that we will prove to ourselves that greatness was always inside.

Morning Manna:

FORWARD EVER BACKWARDS NEVER!!!! As of today make up your mind that you will live in an forward position. What has happened in the pass be it mentally, emotionally, financially and etc. It is vitally important that we get the strength to Let It Go. There are people that have been tough some situations and have not been able to move on because of what has happened in their life. But today make up your mind to move forward. It's not God's will for us to be stuck in regret, pain and despair. A smile on our face but mentally and emotional bankrupt. No joy No inner peace but today make up your mind that you will move forward and enjoy your life. Forward Ever Backwards Never. Have A Life Changing Sunday Worship Experience!!!!!!!!

Morning Manna:

"Lord, let me resist not your Spirit. When I hear your voice, let me move upon it. Even when it's tough and challenging. Open my ears today."

MORNING MANNA:

On today make up in your mind that you will walk into the next phase of your life. And in so doing we must make some decisions to release some people and something's out of our life's. Although it may be painful and hurt to the core. I declare that it is time to walk into that which God has purposed for us. Let's start moving towards the next phase of our life! Shalom

MORNING MANNA:

You don't have time to go over the past, because your now is keeping you busy planning your future. Jer.29:11 GREATER DAYS ARE AHEAD!!!!!!!!!!

MORNING MANNA:

I'msooverit.org Now Moving Forward!!!!!! Let this be your testimony for this Wonderful Wednesday!

MORNING MANNA:

GAURD YOUR TIME!!! Time is so vitally important to our life. We can get money and things back but we can't get time back. When you give people your time you actually give them a portion of your life. GAURD, protect, honor as well as appreciate the time you have. Time is purpose wrapped into the possibilities your realities. I have only just a minute, Only sixty seconds in it. Forced upon me, can't refuse it. Didn't seek it, didn't choose it. But it's up to me to use it. I must suffer if I lose it. Give account if I abuse it. Just a tiny little minute, but eternity is in it. Anonymous

MORNING MANNA:

Our Faith Targets Our Destiny And Our Destiny Awaits Our Faith. Allow your faith to work for you.

MORNING MANNA:

Some people like to tell the truth to everyone but themselves! Truth doesn't work from the outside to in, but rather from the inside out! to thine ownself be true first!

MORNING MANNA:

USE WHAT YOU GOT UNTIL YOU GET WHAT YOU WANT!!!!!! Walking down the street with a loaf of bread the bag in your hand and saying that you are hungry.

MORNING MANNA:

Live A Life Of FAITH Live A Future Of FAITH! Whatever situation, plight or predicament that you find yourself it does not necessarily mean that you did not have faith. Continue To Believe God. That which is to come will be better than that which has been. To God Be The Greater Glory!

MORNING MANNA:

Allow Your Faith To Provide Hope For Someone Who's Around You That May Be Experiencing Some Difficult Times In Their Lives.

MORNING MANNA:

There May Come A Day That I Quit. But Today Will Not Be That Day! Encouragement, Excitement And Enlightenment Is In The Air. Have A Marvelous Monday!

MORNING MANNA:

One Can Very Seldom Get People To Help Pull The Wagon Up A Hill. But Isn't It Ironic That We Can Get Almost

Anyone To Help Push The Wagon Down The Hill. Think About It!!!!!!!!!!!!

MORNING MANNA:

YOU DO BETTER WHEN YOU KNOW BETTER! Dr. Maya Angelo Now is the time to do better, get better and know better. Have a Favorable Friday!

MORNING MANNA:

Assess the situation, count up the cost and make not the good/best decision. But rather make the God lead decision. I declare that life will be better!

MORNING MANNA:

Let us EXAMINE every area of our life to see where we really are. While we are focusing on our strong points, satan is building little pebbles and stones on top of or cover weak areas; and when he attacks, that area is a big mountain of nothingness because we never wanted to deal with it! #dealwithit ... seeing the root of the matter is found in me. Job 19:28 (c)

MORNING MANNA:

MAXIMIZE YOUR FAITH! "Put Your Faith In Over-Drive" This is the season of Divine Opportunity! When FAITH and OPPORTUNITY comes together. It will cause a great Manifestation in your life Faith pulls your OPPORTUNITY "Miracle" towards you. While God Pushes your Manifestation to you. Have A Faith Filled Day!

MORNING MANNA:

WE LIVE IN THIS WORLD Of SADNESS, BUT WE NEED NOT TO LIVE SADLY.

MORNING MANNA:

Everything You See You Don't Need To Talk About. If you see something you don't need to always say something. You need to pray about It. Sometimes just keep your mouth shut.

NOT A SERMON JUST A THOUGHT!

What Is The True Picture Of Our Reality? Is it ours or someone else's? Do we own it or rent it? Are we smiling and there's really is a frown inside? What is our reality. To thine own self be true. Let's no longer fake it but rather FIX it.

Saturday Evening Thought:

Is there anyone that want to give God a praise? Not a praise that's laced with a want or a need but just want to give him praise for being so good.

Saturday Noon Day Meditational Thought

How can the waves of the ocean be separated from the ocean? It can't be. So the Love and Grace of God will never be separated from us. God Loves us with an everlasting Love and guides us with Grace unseen.

AFTERNOON THOUGHT:

"Dear God, give me a spirit of diligence in all tasks, large or small. In doing so, let me set an example for others. Amen." Listen I experienced some unusual FAVOR that was laced with Grace on this morning. Believe God and don't give up. Work your work and stay faithful to God. A $29,000.00 debt reduced to a $50.00 payment. TO GOD BE THE GREATER GLORY!!!!!!!!!!

MIDNIGHT THOUGHT:

PROGRESS SENDS A MESSAGE! NOW LORD ALLOW. ME TO SEND A MESSAGE OF. PROGRESSION...

Random Thought:

Have you ever been forced to stay home and just think about your next move? Weighing the odds exploring the possibilities and counting up the cost. I am getting ready to make a move, God Being My Helper!

Evening Thought:

Face your reality, deal with what you can deal with, handle what you can handle but most of all be secure in yourself. Understand that you owe no man nothing but to love them. strengthen that which concerns you.

EVENING THOUGHT:

No longer my strategies but must strategize through prayer and the word of God!

· SUNDAY MORNING THOUGHT:

ARE WE LIVING OR JUST NEARLY EXISTING? I choose to live! Jesus came that we may have life and that more abundantly. Let's experience life!!!!!!!!!

THIS GOT TO STOP!

I just got finished speaking and encouraging someone Who is really distraught and and hurt over a saint who they thought was their friend. I will never understand the purpose of he say she say. What is the purpose of tearing down ones confidence in an individual or thing. The motive of self-aggrandizement against someone else is wrong, deceitful, petty and demonic. Allow me to remind us what the Bible says about he say she say. The Bible declares that God hates those that sows discord among the brethren.

Whatever you do be real, don't befriend someone and they build confidence in you and you expose them. This need to stop in the body of Christ.

Up, can't sleep, restless got a lot on my mind. Thinking about all the foolish mistakes that I made. Giving my children a better life which they deserve. I am prioritizing my priorities! Rethinking! Refocusing! Reassembling! Rebuilding! LORD HELP ME!

THOUGHT AT NOONDAY:

Get to the point that you start pulling yourself out of the rut. Give GOD something to work with. Mainly yourself.

Just My Thoughts;

I am black... Unapologetically, unabashedly, undecidedly, however not inconsequentially. There's is a constant attack on the skin I was born into... And a second fight rages to deny the first fight is happening. I don't want to debate the merits of gun control, oppression, social justice, legislation or racism as a general concept. I simply want to point out... That 9 people were killed bc they look like me... They could've been me... It is abusive for you to deny that FACT. It is harmful for you to pretend my fears for the lives and safety of my family and friends are unfounded. Race is real... And even if YOU choose not to see it, that doesn't mean it's any less real to me. Now being faced and Challenged with the burning of African American churches. If God Be For Us, Who Can Be Against Us!

While seeking the greater for your life, you must be willing to eliminate some things, some people and some old thoughts. Moving forward in life can be costly but it's worth spending!

NOONDAY THOUGHT:

EVERYTHING RESTS IN THE HAND OF THE LORDS!!!! Put it in his hands.

Have this "1" word ever haunted you? "WHY" Thinking about all of the WHY in my life meaning 1) Why did I do that 2) Why did I say that 3) Why didn't I just pay that 4) Why Why Why Thanking God that Change is Good and that Change is on the Way.

EVENING THOUGHT:

Lord it's been a mighty good day! A mighty good day!

RANDOM THOUGHT:

Is it not something when others need you, you are there, is not it something when people need to talk you are talking to them. But when or if you need them that they are no where around. Or they say they have to be lead by the Lord! Enough Said!!!!

Random Thought at Midnight:

I rather fail a thousand times than to live defeated! Defeat No Longer Defeat Is Not An Option!!!!!

JUST A THOUGHT!

A REAL FRIEND WILL SPEAK REAL TRUTH IN REAL SITUATIONS.

Thanking God for this thing called REBUILDING RETHINKING and RENEWING! The process isn't as hard as I thought, it just takes a mindset to do that which is right.

REBUILDING you must not be afraid of this thing called the process of elimination. Old material can not be used in the new building. RETHINKING develops a new thought process that allows one to REASSES and take another look at things, RENEWING to bring back mending relationships with people that has been damaged hurt and even destroyed. IT'S GETTING BETTER ALL THE TIME!

MORNING THOUGHT. 3:04 a.m. 2015 SHALL BE THE YEAR OF DIVINE EXPLOSION!

Living a life of Divine Discipline and Divine Order. Right Place's Right People and Right Perseptve will bring the expolison

What do you do when your trying isn't good enough and never works out. BUT LORD I HAVE TRIED, I really think that it's time to deal with people like they have dealt with me. I promise this ONE thing that www.MY I DON"T CARE DON"T CARE NOW.com

SATURDAY AFTERNOON:

In the next phase of our lives we must get beyond public opinion and individual thoughts. Never be conformed to the make up of others, but rather transform the thought of others as you define your destiny.***************Live, laugh and love***************

A WORD TO HUSBAND AND SOON TO BE HUSBAND

As I began to reminisce over my marriage that ended in divorce on October 17, 2012, I began to think about the things that I did to cause the divorce. I was lead to share this with you, Hope that you won't judge me but I pray that this will serve as a warning but also encourage you to catch you marriage and take it to the repairer of marriages and that is Jesus. 1) Submit yourselves one to another Although we talk about women submitting but men we must learn to submit to the wife. = giving in, listening realize that we are not always right. 2) Husband love your wife as Christ loved the church = Loving them through ups downs, ins, outs sickness, health and through strong disagreements. 3) And gave himself for it = Please understand that there is nothing to good for YOUR WIFE give her all of you, Give yourself to be a protector for her, shield her from the very attacks. Nowhere in the scripture will you find where the woman is commanded or told to love your husband. I believe that as we love on the woman that God has connected us with the woman will grow in LOVE with you. because what you are showing her. Never take the gift "woman" that God has given you for granted but rather Celebrate, Esteem and promote her. Speak into your life, continue to affirm who she is in your life. Never miss-handle the gift. Watch what you say to her but Love Her Like Christ Love the church But must of all Pray with her, worship with her, cry with her, date her over and over. Hope someone was strengthened and encourage! Bless You.

Friend

HELL IS FOREVER And HEAVEN IS FOR SURE Think About It! GOODNIGHT AND REST WELL!!!

Friend

I AM GRATEFUL TO GOD!!!!!!! IF I Can truthfully Speak and speak with honesty, I have been going through and struggling for the last 2 years. But this week has been the turn around. Thank you Jesus Thank You. GOD HAS A SET TIME TO BRING YOU OUT!

NOT A SERMON JUST MY THOUGHT:

PRAISE Lord I thank you for not Paralyzing my tounge. So on that note I WILL PRAISE YOUR NAME!

NOT A SERMON JUST MY THOUGHT:

LORD I WANT TO HEAR YOUR VOICE CLEARLY, WHILE I FOLLOW YOU CLOSELY! IN GOD I TRUST!

NOT A SERMON JUST MY THOUGHT:

MOVING FROM GOOD TO GREAT! Reexamination, Realigning and Recommitment

NOT A SERMON JUST MY THOUGHT:

Divine order will bring us into our promise and our place of wealth! The year of divine order!

NOT A SERMON JUST MY THOUGHT:

TRUE PRAISE don't shout over Grace and Elevation if you can't shout over Repentance and Forgiveness!

NOT A SERMON JUST MY THOUGHT:

I HAVE BECOME BETTER BECAUSE I HAVE BECOME WISER! Building on my present Expanding my future.

Nov 22

NOT A SERMON JUST MY THOUGHT:

BE YOU! Never allow yourself to fit into framwork of another's opinion of who you should be. BE YOU

NOT A SERMON JUST MY THOUGHT:

I'm getting ready to be ready! Getting ready for my overflow!

NOT A SERMON JUST MY THOUGHT:

There may come a day that i quit, but i declare today isnt that day! God is faithful!

NOT A SERMON JUST MY THOUGHT:

A FAITH THAT HASN'T BEEN TESTED IS A FAITH THAT CAN'T BE TRUSTED. If you make up your mind to go through I declare that God will bring you through!

NOT A SERMON JUST MY THOUGHT:

LIFE BEGINS WHEN YOU DECIDE TO LIVE! Living Unapologetically

NOT A SERMON JUST MY THOUGHT:

Leave it alone! Never live trapped in the mistakes of your yesterday!

NOT A SERMON JUST MY THOUGHT:

THE SEASON OF UNCOMPROMISED CONSISTENCY Stay in your truth, Live in your truth, Speak in your truth.

NOT A SERMON JUST MY THOUGHT:

When We Possess The Attitude Of A Student, We Can Remain Teachable!

NOT A SERMON JUST MY THOUGHT:

WHAT'S TO COME WILL BE BETTER THAN WHAT HAS BEEN! Sometimes in life you must be willing to let things go, so you can appreciate what's to come.

NOT A SERMON JUST MY THOUGHT:

RECOVERY SEASON: Mentally, Emotionally, Spiritually even Financially. We Shall Recover!

NOT A SERMON JUST MY THOUGHT:

EVERYTHING RESTS IN THE HAND OF THE LORD!!!! Put it in his hands.

NOT A SERMON JUST MY THOUGHT:

True Repentance Produces True Humility. The Way To Go Up Is To Go Low.

NOT A SERMON JUST MY THOUGHT:

TO GOD BE THE GREATER GLORY!!!! IN EVERYTHING AND ANYTHING.

NOT A SERMON JUST MY THOUGHT:

STICK WITH WHAT WORKS! Trusting God always has its benefits.

NOT A SERMON JUST MY THOUGHT:

Lord I don't want to be in POSITION with no POWER! But rather POWER with NO POSITION.

NOT A SERMON JUST MY THOUGHT:

PREPARATION IS EVERYTHING! If you fail to plan, then you plan to fail.

NOT A SERMON JUST MY THOUGHT:

Prepared and Positioned To Receive The Promise!

NOT A SERMON JUST MY THOUGHT:

God had the solution to the problem, before you knew there was a problem.

NOT A SERMON JUST MY THOUGHT:

Faith living! Believe it you'll receive it, but if you doubt it you'll do without it!

NOT A SERMON JUST MY THOUGHT:

Never entertain a lie and never allow a lie to arrest your time! Keep on living!

NOT A SERMON JUST MY THOUGHT:

FORWARD LIVING! Don't allow anyone or anything to make you or persuade you to go against the principles that you have set for yourself. Make Rules For Yourself And Live By Them!!!

NOT A SERMON JUST MY THOUGHT:

Your absence will validates your presence. Know who you are and Know your worth.

NOT A SERMON JUST MY THOUGHT:

EXCEEDING EXPECTATIONS! Nothing Missing, Nothing Broken, Nothing Lacking THE YEAR OF DIVINE ORDER!

NOT A SERMON JUST MY THOUGHT:

2019 THE YEAR OF PRODUCTIVITY! We will not be able to conceptualize the favor that we will walk in.

NOT A SERMON JUST MY THOUGHT:

THE SAFEST PLACE IN THE WHOLE WORLD IS IN THE WILL OF GOD! Where are you?

NOT A SERMON JUST MY THOUGHT:

YOU ARE SIGNIFICANT! Regardless of the situation that you find yourself wrestling with know that you are a person of great importance

NOT A SERMON JUST MY THOUGHT:

STEP BACK AND THINK THINGS THROUGH. Take time to assess those that are around you and whom you make yourself accessible to. Because you are accessible to them does not mean that they respect or celebrate you. It could be that you are just being tolerated. Stop and take notice of how they entreat you and then how they entreat someone else. KNOW YOUR WORTH AND WHAT YOU BRING TO ANY SITUATION. SOMETIMES YOU JUST GOT TO REMOVE YOURSELF FROM THE EQUATION.

NOT A SERMON JUST MY THOUGHT:

Are we so falsely lead by religion until we miss out on a relationship with God!

NOT A SERMON JUST MY THOUGHT:

DON'T SETTLE Hold up and don't give up Your blessing is sure to come. Don't Settle

A SERMON JUST MY THOUGHT:

SELF ACCOUNTABILITY It's always easier to blame someone else in the situation but sometimes we must be accountable for our own actions. When you see someone that's always saying it was them, they did, we didn't and never take the onus of their action but would rather play the victim that is one who have not become self accountable. Let's begin to take accountability for our actions and things that we didn't do that we should have done. Let's repent for deceiving ourselves and lying on and to others and then God will apply his grace then we can move in PRODUCTIVITY!

NOT A SERMON JUST MY THOUGHT:

Don't allow the trouble to trouble you, but rather trouble your trouble!

NOT A SERMON JUST MY THOUGHT:

Love god with all of your heart, love yourself unconditionally, live your life unapologetic!

NOT A SERMON JUST MY THOUGHT:

A going church for a coming lord! Will you be able and ready?

NOT A SERMON JUST MY THOUGHT:

IT'S WORKING Romans 8:28 Don't give in, don't give up, don't throw in the towel.

NOT A SERMON JUST MY THOUGHT:

A HIGH PRAISE IN YOUR LOW PLACE! In your life difficulties or pain. Just give a God High Praise.

NOT A SERMON JUST MY THOUGHT:

DIVINE ORDER!!! "It will take you to a place where you have never been before! Let's live it.

NOT A SERMON JUST MY THOUGHT:

STEP BACK AND WATCH!!! Life has a way of proving it's self being good, bad or indifferent. In life we must step back to examine who's around us and what we have involved ourselves in. Step back and examine how your life have been going since you have been involved in that situation or with that individual. Change Is Not Change Until You Make The Change!!!!!!!

NOT A SERMON JUST MY THOUGHT:

HEAVEN IS NOT BROKE AND THE ANGELS ARE NOT ON WELFARE! Believe God and will work it out!

NOT A SERMON JUST MY THOUGHT:

Life is like a camera, focus on what is important, capture the good times, develop from the negatives, and if things don't work out, just take another shot. Have A Sensational Saturday!

NOT A SERMON JUST MY THOUGHT:

DON'T COMPROMISE THE INTEGRITY OF THE PROCESS! Don't get distracted by the process of change. Stay until the change is complete!! Once transformed, you'll never go back.... A butterfly can't go back to a caterpillar!

NOT A SERMON JUST MY THOUGHT:

RIGHT! Let's live right, Let's do right Let's do ministry right. Right will out live wrong any day.

NOT A SERMON JUST MY THOUGHT:

MOVING FORWARD UNAPOLOGETICALLY, UNASHAMEDLY WITHOUT REGRET. Never live your life on the thoughts of someone else, but rather define your own destiny. Live and be happy, Live and enjoy. But most of all lets live a life of Holiness and

Wholeness!!! Life is here today and gone today. Let's live! 2019 THE YEAR OF PRODUCTIVITY!

NOT A SERMON JUST MY THOUGHT!

MESSAGE THIS MORNING IS THROUGH SONG. ENJOY!

Set Apart and Chosen's post

The Lord Will Make A Way | Maggie Ingram and Meta Miller Set Apart and Chosen is now on Instagram! Follow us... http://www.instagram.com/setapartandchosen1

Jun 21

NOT A SERMON JUST MY THOUGHT:

NEVER ALLOW THE MISTAKES OF YOUR YESTERDAY TO CRIPPLE YOUR TODAY. Phil. 3:13-14 MOVE FORWARD!

NOT A SERMON JUST MY THOUGHT:

PREPARATION IS EVERYTHING! There's No Short Cuts To Success.

NOT A SERMON JUST MY THOUGHT:

If You Hold Up And Don't Give Up GOD Will Show Up!

NOT A SERMON JUST MY THOUGHT:

HOW ARE YOU LIVING? HOLINESS is still the order of the day!!!

NOT A SERMON JUST MY THOUGHT:

NO SAD STORY! I'm just grateful that God has kept me through everything.

NOT A SERMON JUST MY THOUGHT:

PRAISE! Lord I thank you for not Paralyzing my tongue. So for that I WILL PRAISE YOUR NAME!

NOT A SERMON JUST MY THOUGHT:

I'M WALKING THIS THING OUT!!! F.A.I.T.H F-FORSAKING A-ALL I-I T-TRUST H-HIM

NOT A SERMON JUST MY THOUGHT:

LOVE ON PURPOSE! LOVE ISN'T LOVE UNLESS YOU GIVE IT AWAY!

NOT A SERMON JUST MY THOUGHT:

I GOTTA HAVE IT! My peace is essential to my existence

NOT A SERMON JUST MY THOUGHT:

A FAITH THAT HASN'T BEEN TESTED, IS A FAITH THAT CAN'T BE TRUSTED. If you make up your mind to go through I declare that God will bring you through!

NOT A SERMON JUST MY THOUGHT:

WE ARE SURVIVORS! God may not deliver us out of our situation but God will step into our situations.

NOT A SERMON JUST MY THOUGHT:

SIN IS STILL SIN "REPENT" When you turn then God will turn it!

NOT A SERMON JUST MY THOUGHT:

LOVE UNFAILING How can the waves of the ocean be separated from the ocean? It can't be. So the Love and Grace of God will never be separated from us. God Loves us with an everlasting Love and guides us with Grace unseen.

NOT A SERMON JUST MY THOUGHT:

God EasesThe Pain While We Discover New Possibilities! "LET'S GO "

NOT A SERMON JUST MY THOUGHT:

SPEAK WISELY! What remains unsaid, never needs an apology. ⍰

NOT A SERMON JUST MY THOUGHT:

SEEK GOD! Every good idea doesn't mean that it's a God idea. Proverbs 3:5-7

NOT A SERMON JUST MY THOUGHT:

ALTHOUGH IT MAY BE ROUGH, IT MAY BE NECESSARY. While it may hurt and be painful. Perplexing and disturbing. Don't give up because God is strengthening and developing you, and he will get the Glory.

NOT A SERMON JUST A THOUGHT:

KEEP YOUR PEACE! You got to know when to let go and walk away.

NOT A SERMON JUST MY THOUGHT:

Don't let a few seconds of satisfaction "of any sort" sabotage your season of success.

NOT A SERMON JUST MY THOUGHT:

A person that have a problem committing, will always have a problem submitting.

NOT A SERMON JUST MY THOUGHT:

GROW THROUGH WHAT YOU GO THROUGH! Life has a way of throwing us a few curve balls, and uncertainties have attempted to arrest our mind. Life is a one way street, from the cradle to the grave. There's no time outs there's no intermission but it's a steady progression from the Date of Birth until The Date of Death. Whatever the situation may be in your life know that it is a lesson to be learned. It may be painful but endure the lesson. God will strengthen us, God will guide us and God will uphold us through it all. Grow through it.

NOT A SERMON JUST MY THOUGHT:

SILENCE IS GOLDEN!!! Stop talking your business and just handle your business. Just let people see the progress/change. People don't know what you don't tell. And people can't doubt what you don't reveal. SILENCE IS GOLDEN!!!

NOT A SERMON JUST MY THOUGHT:

Get To A Place Where Your Prayers Can Be Heard, And Mercies Can Be Found.

NOT A SERMON JUST MY THOUGHT:

What remains unsaid, never needs an apology. Let's Speak wisely!

NOT A SERMON JUST MY THOUGHT:

FORWARD EVER In order to move forward in life we must first accept and deal with our present. Sometimes our now can be so painful and hurtful that's it's hard to really move forward.

We have to make up our mind that we will not dance over it anymore we will not speak in tongues over it anymore would no longer do anymore spiritual calisthenics to try to make the pain go away. But what we will do is make up our mind to confront it, deal with it and move FORWARD. Life Is Worth Living And We Shall Live!

NOT A SERMON JUST MY THOUGHT:

Never keep making yourself available for those who continuously make themselves unavailable to you.

NOT A SERMON JUST MY THOUGHT:

NO EXCEPTIONS! Joy is yours to claim, Destiny is yours to secure and Peace is yours to walk in. Forgetting your past celebrate your now and prepare to enjoy your future. MOVING FORWARD WITHOUT ANY EXCEPTIONS!

NOT A SERMON JUST MY THOUGHT:

LEAP OF FAITH! Your DESTINY is awaiting your faith move.

NOT A SERMON JUST MY THOUGHT:

JUST GRACE! Lord I'm thankful for your Grace. It keeps us, it covers us, it protects us.

NOT A SERMON JUST MY THOUGHT:

STAY LOW The highest position that I want to go is at the feet of JESUS!

NOT A SERMON JUST MY THOUGHT:

IF YOU CAN'T AFFORD TO GIVE IT AWAY THEN YOU PROBABLY CAN'T AFFORD TO KEEP IT. Love isn't love unless you can give it away.

NOT A SERMON JUST MY THOUGHT:

Watch who you allow to ring the bell for you, once the Bell have been rung it can't be unrung.

NOT A SERMON JUST MY THOUGHT:

HOLD ON! God will bring us out of despair, and bring us into a place of peace and promise.

NOT A SERMON JUST MY THOUGHT:

GOD ALTERS YOUR LIFE PLANNED EVENTS! Have you ever had anything planned and you was in pursuit of it? To find what you planned is not your plans any longer. Have you ever planned a certain career and was working on it? Just to find yourself in a total different career. Have you ever said that you wasn't going to do something? But you find yourself doing that which you said you wouldn't do.

GOD ALTERS YOUR LIFE PLANNED EVENTS!

NOT A SERMON JUST MY THOUGHT:

A PURPOSE BEHIND OUR PROBLEM! As of today look at your problems in a different way. Understand the problems that you are facing can be used to propel you into the purpose that God has for your life Don't dismiss your pain but deal with it. Examine your problem and pursue your God-given purpose

NOT A SERMON JUST MY THOUGHT:

THIS IS WHY YOU CAN'T HEAR ME! Sometimes your greatest speak is no speak at all! Your silence speaks more clearer then that of your speak. There are times when you just need to be quiet!

NOT A SERMON JUST MY THOUGHT:

SEED DAY! Let today be the day that you bless someone. Buy them a meal, Cash app them do something tangible for someone. When I awoke this morning and was pondering what should my Not A Sermon Just My Thought be about today the Lord spoke to me and said SEED DAY. Take time to bless someone today, a friend, co worker, family or someone you dont know. Bless Someone today I'm going to do it as well.

NOT A SERMON JUST MY THOUGHT:

HOW ARE YOU LIVING? Holiness is still right and it is the order of the day.

NOT A SERMON JUST MY THOUGHT:

While seeking the greater for your life, you must be willing to eliminate some things, some people and some old thoughts. Moving forward in life can be costly but it's worth spending! GREATER IS COMING!

NOT A SERMON JUST MY THOUGHT:

GOD GOT IT ALL IN CONTROL! Trust him totally to navigate you through your situation. Jer. 29:11

NOT A SERMON JUST MY THOUGHT:

THE TRUTH NEEDS NO JUSTIFICATION. Talk it, Walk it and Live it!

NOT A SERMON JUST MY THOUGHT:

UNCERTAIN OF THE CERTAINTY! When you know God said a thing, continue to believe through hard times.

NOT A SERMON JUST MY THOUGHT:

God's Blessings Are Greater Than Any Of Life's Burdens. God Has A SET Time To Bring You Out!!!

NOT A SERMON JUST MY THOUGHT:

KEEP LOOKING UP IT'S GOT TO GET BETTER! There's a bright side somewhere. Don't stop looking.

NOT A SERMON JUST MY THOUGHT:

Don't allow people who are supposed to be on the balcony to sit on your front row.

NOT A SERMON JUST MY THOUGHT:

STAND TOGETHER! It's Cold When You Are Standing By Yourself! And it's frigid when you're all alone.

Nov 18

NOT A SERMON JUST MY THOUGHT:

KNOW WHO YOU ARE! Just because others don't see your WHY/PURPOSE don't mean you don't have one. Jesse had a king in his house named David, and didn't even know it.

NOT A SERMON JUST MY THOUGHT:

When moving in a New Direction you must leave your present address! Somethings must be left behind.

NOT A SERMON JUST MY THOUGHT:

PLEASE AND THANK YOU! I would rather someone tell me the ugly truth, than a pretty lie. Am I not your friend because I told you the truth?

NOT A SERMON JUST MY THOUGHT:

Take Inventory Of Your Surroundings. Releasing people and starting over is sometimes a good thing!

NOT A SERMON JUST MY THOUGHT:

GIVE GOD A HIGH PRAISE IN YOUR LOW PLACE! I'll Bless The Lord At All Times... Ps 34:1

NOT A SERMON JUST MY THOUGHT:

BREAK THE BOX

Never live life through the FRAMWORK or the LENS of another person.

But rather give definition to who you are and will be.

NOT A SERMON JUST MY THOUGHT:

MOVE BEYOND YOUR NOW!

Life will throw many curveballs our way as we find ourselves im vicarious situation. Although we may have to stop but we can't get stuck, remember we must move beyond our present situation and daily drama and face the mistakes of our past secure the reality of our now while we move for our brighter tomorrow.

BETTER DAYS AHEAD!

NOT A SERMON JUST MY THOUGHT:

I'VE GOT TO GET MYSELF TOGETHER WEALTH BUILDING"

"ECONOMIC DEVELOPMENT!"

Get it. Keep it. Put it away. Generate as much income as you can and put it away to invest in income-producing assets.

To put it together, you have understand how income flows work. Most people rely on one flow of income like a salary. Salaries are a hammock -- a place where you sit back and enjoy if it's good enough. Sounds nice, but what do you do when something unexpected happens? Just like the ups and downs of the economy, you have to plan for the worst.

Look for ways to increase your main flow of income and build as many secondary flows that you can. When you're looking to move from one flow to the next, make sure they are symbiotic and reinforce what you're already doing. Too many people pay attention to a secondary flow and let go of the first one. Always protect your main flow and use it to fuel all others.

Just because things appear to be going well, you have to be prepared for the worst. If you have no money, don't blame the economy. Go to sleep like your broke. Wake up hungry. Get ready. Stay ready. Build up your personal economy to such massive levels that no economic event can take it away from you.

NOT A SERMON JUST MY THOUGHT:

WATCH YOUR MOUTH!

Never Tell Anyone Anything That You Would Want Them To FORGIVE.

NOT A SERMON JUST MY THOUGHT:

MOVING BEYOND

So focused on where I'm going to the point where I came from doesn't matter anymore.

NOT A SERMON JUST MY THOUGHT:

SILENCE IS GOLDEN!!!

Stop talking your business and just handle your business. Just let people see the progress/change.

People don't know what you don't tell. And people can't doubt what you don't reveal.

SILENCE IS GOLDEN!!!

NOT A SERMON JUST MY THOUGHT :

WATCH YOUR MOUTH!

What remains unsaid, never needs an apology. Speak wisely...

NOT A SERMON JUST MY THOUGHT:

JESUS HEALS THROUGH OUR PRIVATE PAIN.

Matters not what it is, we all have private matters that we're dealing with

Let Jesus HEAL You

NOT A SERMON JUST MY THOUGHT:

SIN IS LIKE A BED IT'S EASY TO GET INTO BUT HARD TO GET OUT OF!

It's hard but get out of it.

NOT A SERMON JUST MY THOUGHT:

STOP TELLING PEOPLE WHERE YOU ARE GOING, BUT RATHER START TELLING THEM WHERE YOU HAVE BEEN.

In other words don't tell people what you are going to do but what you have done.

NOT A SERMON JUST MY THOUGHT:

The Hand Of God Will Hold Us And Guide Us Until Times Gets Better! "Don't Compromise The Process!"

NOT A SERMON JUST MY THOUGHT:

I HAVE BECOME BETTER, BECAUSE I HAVE BECOME WISER! Building on my present to expand my future.

NOT A SERMON JUST MY THOUGHT:

OH GOD I THANK YOU! I Just felt like telling the Lord THANK YOU.

NOT A SERMON JUST MY THOUGHT:

"YOU SURVIVED IT! Things had happened, pain was inflicted, marriages ended in divorce and even health has become challenged. Finances dried up, children went out of control, the person the you loved died. Lost your home, car broke down or even repossessed. Whatever your plight know that YOU SURVIVED!!!!!!

NOT A SERMON JUST MY THOUGHT:

BUILD YOU AND BUILD YOUR BRAND. While pushing and supporting someone else's vision or work don't forget or bury the vision that's inside thats need to be birthed or built. People work on that ministry, work on that business, work on that book, work on that family. This is the TIME and SEASON to be began to build. BUILD BUILD BUILD

NOT A SERMON JUST MY THOUGHT:

NOTHING BUT THE TRUTH Because you don't like a situation, don't change the truth of the situation. Be angry be upset but understand the truth REEMAINS the SAME. You cannot manipulate it you cannot fool it and really you can't contaminate it. The truth is the truth all day long. What is the truth of your Reality?

NOT A SERMON JUST MY THOUGHT:

Satan uses our natural to effect our spiritual, but God uses our spiritual to effect our natural. Our spiritual covers, guides and protects us from all hurt harm or danger. Satan subtracts and divides while God ADDS and MULTIPLIES

NOT A SERMON JUST MY THOUGHT:

GOD WILL GUIDE US AND GAURD US! In him only do we safely trust and rely upon.

NOT A SERMON JUST MY THOUGHT:

As long as you know your value and your worth, NO one can devalue you or make you feel worthless. Love yourself!

NOT A SERMON JUST MY THOUGHT: MOVING FORWARD WITHOUT ANY FURTHER DELAYS. DESTINY AWAITS US!

NOT A SERMON JUST MY THOUGHT: Through Your Life's Story, Don't Ever Forget To Give God The Glory!

NOT A SERMON JUST MY THOUGHT: I'VE GOT TO GET MYSELF TOGETHER WEALTH BUILDING" "ECONOMIC DEVELOPMENT!" Get it. Keep it. Put it away. Generate as much income as you can and put it away to invest in income-producing assets. To put it together, you have understand how income flows work. Most people rely on one flow of income like a salary. Salaries are a hammock -- a place where you sit back and enjoy if it's good enough. Sounds nice, but what do you do when something unexpected happens? Just like the ups and downs of the economy, you have to plan for the worst. Look for ways to increase your main flow of income and build as many secondary flows that you can. When you're looking to move from one flow to the next, make sure they are symbiotic and reinforce what you're already doing. Too many people pay attention to a secondary flow and let go of the first one. Always protect your main flow and use it to fuel all others Just because things appear to be going well, you have to be prepared for the worst. If you have no money, don't blame the economy. Go to sleep like your broke. Wake up hungry. Get ready. Stay ready. Build up your personal economy to such massive levels that no economic event can take it away from you.

NOT A SERMON JUST MY THOUGHT:

FALL BACK SO YOU CAN GO FORWARD! In order to go forward in life, sometimes we must back up to reassess, realign and refocus.

NOT A SERMON JUST MY THOUGHT:

Sometime as you step back and remove yourself from the equation it's only then that you can see the TRUE heart of a person. NEVER allow anyone to taint your perception or mindset when you know the truth. INTEGRITY IS THE FRAME-WORK WHILE CHARACTER BUILDS UPON IT!

NOT A SERMON JUST MY THOUGHT:

KNOW WHO YOU ARE!!!!! Just because others don't see your WHY/PURPOSE don't mean you don't have one. "Jesse had a king living in his house named David,"

NOT A SERMON JUST MY THOUGHT:

Allow Your Absence To VALIDATE Your Presence. Why be tolerated when you can be celebrated? ⁉️

NOT A SERMON JUST MY THOUGHT:

I GOTTA HAVE IT! Know that your PEACE is essential to your existence.

NOT A SERMON JUST MY THOUGHT:

ADDITION THROUGH SUBTRACTION Sometimes we have to give it up, to build up.

NOT A SERMON JUST MY THOUGHT:

THE RIGHTEOUS NEED NOT TO HOLD UP A FLAG. When one have made a mistake you need not to show your spiritual trophy case but rather show love and restoration.

NOT A SERMON JUST MY LTHOUGHT:

BETTER! ON THE HORIZON! Before we can expect Better Living we must accept our present reality. Once we own our reality then we can begin to make changes for the better Your present position don't have to do your permanent placement!

NOT A SERMON JUST MY THOUGHT:

ARE YOU READY? Prepared and positioned to receive the promise.

NOT A SERMON JUST MY THOUGHT:

LIVE FOR YOU AND NOT OHTHER'S Your greatness will not always fit into others views of you. Stop trying to fit your square peg into other people's round space. Keep being great no matter what...

NOT A SERMON JUST MY THOUGHT:

People may talk about you, but after a while they'll change their conversation and talk about something else. It will wear off so keep pushing.

NOT A SERMON JUST MY THOUGHT:

JESUS HEALS THROUGH OUR PRIVATE PAIN. Matters not what it is, we all have private matters that we're dealing with Let Jesus HEAL You

NOT A SERMON JUST A THOUGHT:

Never allow your response to someone's comment reduce you to the ignorance of the person who made the comment. Good Wednesday Morning!

NOT A SERMON JUST MY THOUGHT:

"CHANGE RENDERS RESULTS" If we want change in our lives we then sometimes must make some radical changes within ourselves. Change requires Discipline, Discipline requires Determination, Determination requires Direction to know where you want to go in your change. Change is ours to Claim. Change can be done.

NOT A SERMON JUST MY THOUGHT!

FRUSTRATE THE FRUSTRATOR! When he want you to go down You continue to get up.

NOT A SERMON JUST MY THOUGHT:

GOD HAD THE SOLUTION TO THE PROBLEM, BEFORE WE KNEW THERE WAS A PROBLEM.

NOT A SERMON JUST MY THOUGHT:

I'M GETTING READY TO BE READY! GETTING READY FOR MY OVERFLOW!

NOT A SERMON JUST MY THOUGHT:

PRACTICAL PREPARATION FOR SPIRITUAL MANISFESTATION! You must have a plan and a vision.

NOT A SERMON JUST MY THOUGHT:

LIFE IS A CAMERA! Focus on what is important, Capture the good times, Develop from the negatives, and if things don't work out, Adjust your lens and just take another shot.

NOT A SERMON JUST MY THOUGHT:

Enjoy The Ride! It's not just the destination that's Important, but it's the adventure that goes along with the ride.

NOT A SERMON JUST MY THOUGHT:

TRUTHFUL FRIENDS! Am I therefore become your enemy, because I tell you the truth... Galatians 4:16 Never compromise a friendship with someone because he/she has spoke truth to you or your situation.

NOT A SERMON JUST MY THOUGHT:

Our Faith Targets Our Destiny And Our Destiny Awaits Our Faith. Allow your faith to work for you.

NOT A SERMON JUST MY THOUGHT:

IF NOT NOW THEN WHEN? Let's make up our mind that we will suffer no more delay. DESTINY AWAITS!

NOT A SERMON JUST MY THOUGHT:

HELL IS TO HOT AND ETERNITY IS TO LONG! Why not live right?

NOT A SERMON JUST MY THOUGHT:

SEED DAY! LOVE ISN'T LOVE UNLESS YOU CAN GIVE IT AWAY. Let today be the day that you bless someone. Buy them a meal, Cash app them do something tangible for someone. When I awoke this morning and was pondering what should my Not A Sermon Just My Thought be about today the Lord spoke to me and said SEED DAY. Take time to bless someone today, Bless Someone today I'm going to do it as well. Drop your cash app. I may bless someone from the cash or in person.

NOT A SERMON JUST MY THOUGHT:

HOW DOES YOUR ACCOUNT LOOK? If you continue to allow people to make more withdrawals in your life than deposits, you will be overdrawn and living in a negative balance. Know when to close your account. **THIS IS THE SEASON TO LIVE IN SURPLUS** I have closed some accounts "relationships" Nothing from Nothing = Nothing No More Negativity!

NOT A SERMON JUST MY THOUGHT:

I'M IN A SEASON OF MY LIFE WHERE I JUST WON'T DEAL WITH DISTRACTIONS!

NOT A SERMON JUST MY THOUGHT:

LIVING IN DIVINE ORDER! Gifts and talents do not exalt us above personal responsibility.

NOT A SERMON JUST MY THOUGHT:

JUST DO IT! Doing the GODLY thing will always be the GODLY thing to do.

NOT A SERMON JUST MY THOUGHT:

MAKE TODAY COUNT! Today is a day for a good day!

NOT A SERMON JUST MY THOUGHT:

A Spoken Truth Is Better Than A Secret Lie. Speak Truth!

NOT A SERMON JUST MY THOUGHT:

Every Good Idea Isn't A GOD IDEA! Seek GODLY counsel with your good idea.

NOT A SERMON JUST MY THOUGHT:

Never Allow Anyone Who Don't Know Their Assignment, To Move You Out Of Your Assignment!! Good Saturday Morning!

NOT A SERMON JUST MY THOUGHT:

GOOD TO GREAT Re-Assessing, Re-Focusing and Re-Enforcing Taking the limits off God! Psalms 78:41

Made in the USA
Middletown, DE
21 December 2024

68031225R00109